D1565575

THE MAKE
YOUR OWN
JOKE
B K

First published in 2006 as *It's True! You can make your own jokes*

Allen & Unwin
83 Alexander Street
Crows Nest NSW 2065
Australia
  Phone (612) 8425 0100
    Fax (612) 9906 2218
  Email info@allenandunwin.com
   Web www.allenandunwin.com

National Library of Australia Cataloguing-in-Publication entry:
  Holt, Sharon.
  The make-your-own joke book / Sharon Holt ;
    illustrator, Ross Kinnaird.
  ISBN 978 174175 582 4 (pbk.)
  For primary school age. Wit and humour, Juvenile.

808.7

This book is printed on FSC-certified
paper. The printer holds FSC chain of
custody SGS-COC-004121. The FSC promotes
environmentally responsible, socially
beneficial and economically viable
management of the worlds forests.

Text and cover design by Bruno Herfst
Set in 11/15 pt Legacy Sans
Printed in Australia by McPherson's Printing Group

10 9 8 7 6 5 4 3 2 1

*When I was younger, I asked my dad
why people smiled at me when they walked by.
'Because it's rude to laugh,' he replied.*

This book's for you, Dad.

CONTENTS

1 JUST JOKING

7 KNOCK-OUTS AND SIDE-SPLITS

20 CRAZY CACKLE-A-THON

25 CLOWNING AROUND

32 INVENT-A-WORD

44 PRANKS AND HOAXES

51 ALL MIXED UP

61 BRAIN TWISTERS

70 LAUGHERS LIVE LONGER

76 THE LAST LAUGH

JUST JOKING

Q Why do French people eat snails?

A *Because they don't like fast food.*

Q What did the fly say when the bee asked it out on a date?

A *Buzz off!*

The World's First Joke

Have you ever wondered who told the first joke? Joking is mentioned in the Bible, but one of the first joke books was written by a Greek funny man named Hierocles in about 500 CE. It was called *The Philogelos*, or 'Laughter-Lover'. Here's one: 'How shall I cut your hair?' said a talkative barber to his customer. 'In silence!' was the reply.

Jest books were very popular in Europe in the Middle Ages, when times were tough and a good chuckle helped lift the mood after a particularly gruesome series of battles and executions.

The World's Funniest Joke

In 2002, an important internet experiment was conducted – people were invited to submit their favourite jokes. More than 40 000 jokes were collected, and then people voted for the funniest. Two million votes later, this was the winner:

The world's funniest yolk

Two hunters are out in the woods when one of them collapses. He doesn't seem to be breathing and his eyes are glazed. The other guy takes out his phone and calls the emergency services. He gasps, 'My friend is dead! What can I do?' The operator says, 'Calm down. First, let's make sure he's dead.' There is silence, then a gunshot is heard. Back on the phone, the guy says, 'Okay, now what?'

Who Put the Punch in Punchline?

The end of a joke is called the **punchline**. It's a phrase that's been around since the early 1920s. Television hadn't been invented then, and people enjoyed watching vaudeville shows that were full of wisecracks and pranks.

Jokes were often acted out by two performers – a 'funny man' and a 'straight man'. The funny man played pranks on the straight man, who always kept a straight face, no matter what was going on. At the end of a gag, the funny man pretended to punch the straight man – hence 'punchline' for the climax of a joke.

Who Put the Pun in Punch?

The secret of joke-writing is knowing where to start. And guess what – it's not at the beginning!

The best way to make up a joke is to know how it ends. If you can figure out a good punchline, you're nearly there.

Punchlines hold the key to great gags for another reason. A **pun** is a play on words that sound or look the same. Take 'sail' and 'sale', for example: the words sound the same but have different meanings. It's the same with words like 'pause' and 'paws'.

Q When is the best time to buy a yacht?

A *When it's on sale.*

Q How do you keep a cat quiet?

A *Push the paws.*

Keep an ear out for all those words that sound the same but have different meanings, and you'll really start to see the punny side of life!

It's All About the Timing

It's important to pick the right moment to tell your joke. If people feel happy, they'll probably laugh out loud. If they feel sad, a joke could cheer them up. But if they feel angry, it might be best to wait until they've cooled down.

If you think a joke is funny, chances are that other people your age will find it funny too. Younger people may not understand it. Older people may find it silly.

Finally, try not to tell a really unfunny joke!

KNOCK-OUTS AND SIDE-SPLITS

The world wouldn't be the same without **knock-knock** jokes. They'll get a laugh from both young kids and adults because they're easy to understand and create a funny mental image. And knock-knock jokes follow a pattern, so they're easy to remember.

Look at these two examples:

> **Knock knock**
> *Who's there?*
> **Snow.**
> *Snow who?*
> **Snow time for jokes – just open the door!**

> **Knock knock**
> *Who's there?*
> **Shirley.**
> *Shirley who?*
> **Shirley you recognise your own mother!**

Why Do We Laugh?

These knock-knock jokes work because the name of the person knocking at the door sounds like another word. 'Shirley' sounds like 'Surely' and 'Snow' sounds like 'It's no'.

As with all jokes, the key is in the punchline. You expect to hear someone's name when you ask, 'Who's there?' You don't expect the name to be the start of a whole sentence, so your mind is tricked and the name you hear turns out to have a different meaning. Ideally, the punchline is something you might say as you come through a doorway. For example, if the end of the second joke was, 'Shirley you like custard,' it wouldn't work as well.

Still Knocking

Knock knock
Who's there?
Albert.
Albert who?
Albert a million bucks
you can't guess who's knocking.

Knock knock
Who's there?
Daryl.
Daryl who?
Daryl be trouble
if you don't open dis door soon.

Knock knock
Who's there?
Venice.
Venice who?
Venice dis door going to be opened?

Knock knock
Who's there?
Kenya.
Kenya who?
Kenya please open the door?

MAKE YOUR OWN
KNOCK-KNOCK JOKES

Write a list of names on a piece of scrap paper.
Here are some ideas:

- People you know
- Names in magazines or newspapers
- Names from TV programs

Take another piece of paper.

Head it up at the top like this:

LIST A   LIST B

Look at your list of names. Say each name to yourself. When you find a name that sounds like another word, write the name in List A. Write the word it sounds like in List B.

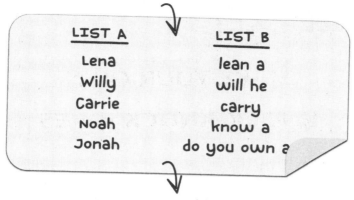

LIST A	LIST B
Lena	lean a
Willy	will he
Carrie	carry
Noah	know a
Jonah	do you own ?

All knock-knock jokes follow this pattern:

Knock knock
Who's there?
....
.... *who?*
Punchline

Use one of your names from List A to fill in the gaps. When you get to the punchline, find a funny ending for the List B word or phrase. For example, the 'Jonah' joke might end:

'Jonah red sports car? Better run,
it's rolling down the hill.'

Use the lists to make up more jokes. You can also use surnames, cities, countries, animals and food in List A.

SIDE-SPLITS

Now that you've warmed up with these knock-knock jokes, let's try some **side-splits**. Here are two examples:

Q What part of a window hurts the most?

A *The window pane.*

Q What card game do you play in hospital?

A *Patience.*

Why Do We Laugh?

Side-splits are jokes that use puns or words with double meanings to get a laugh. In these examples, the puns are 'pane' and 'pain' and 'patience' and 'patients'. The question in a side-split always gives clues to the answer. The word 'hurt' is the clue in the first joke and 'card game' is the clue in the second joke.

Luckily for the joker, the English language is full of words that sound the same but have different meanings. You can even write more than one joke using the same pair of words!

Side-splitters

Q **What do you eat while you're driving?**

A *Traffic jam.*

Q **Why didn't the chicken have a job?**

A *Because she kept getting laid off.*

I hate chicken jokes!

Q **Why couldn't the piece of wood find anything to do?**

A *Because he was a little board.*

Q **Why didn't the man take any money to the public pool?**

A *Because he wanted to swim freestyle.*

Q **What part of a book is the happiest?**

A *The contents.*

MAKE YOUR OWN
SIDE-SPLIT JOKES

Use a dictionary to find words that sound the same but have different meanings. (The spelling can be the same or different.) Choose three words that have several meanings. Call this 'List A'.

For example:

LIST A

Court: Where a judge works
       Place for playing sports

Space: Open space
       Outer space

Trunk: Tree trunk
       Elephant's trunk
       Storage box

Look at each set of words you have chosen. Try to find a way of linking the two meanings with a question. Some words will easily make jokes. Others will take time. If you get stuck, choose another set of words.

Here are three examples using words from List A:

Q Where do they send bad basketball players?

A *To court.*

Q Why did the astronaut move to a bigger house?

A *He wanted more space.*

Q Where does an elephant store his belongings?

A *In his trunk.*

Side-splitting Sports Specials

Are you crazy about sports? You could go crazy making up side-split jokes about sports and games from shuttlecock to snooker!

Q Which piece of sports equipment makes the most noise?

A *A racquet.*

Q What game do you play if you leave your boots at home?

A *Sock-er.*

Q What kind of jewellery do gymnasts prefer?

A *Rings.*

Yet another chicken joke

Q Why wasn't the chicken allowed to play basketball?

A *Because there were no fouls allowed.*

Q **What did the baseball fan give his girlfriend for her birthday?**

A *A diamond.*

Q **What do basketball players do with their biscuits?**

A *Dunk them.*

Q **How did the tennis ball become a squash ball?**

A *It sat on the road.*

Q **How old do you have to be to play tennis?**

A *Tennish.*

MAKE YOUR OWN
SPORTS JOKES

Think of a sport you know well because you play or watch it often.

List all the words you can think of that are used in that sport. Call this 'List A'.

Here's an example for soccer:

LIST A

Ball
Shoot
Dribble

Some of the words in List A may have two meanings. They may also sound like another word with a different meaning; 'court' and 'caught', for example. Start a 'List B' and write down any

**different meanings for the sporting words in
List A. Use a dictionary if you need some help.**

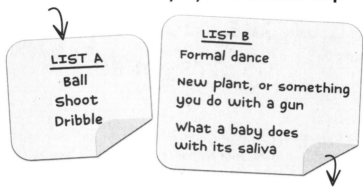

LIST A
- Ball
- Shoot
- Dribble

LIST B
Formal dance

New plant, or something
you do with a gun

What a baby does
with its saliva

**Choose one of your word pairs from List A and B.
Think of a way to link the meanings. Use the two
meanings to write a joke.**

Here are two examples using 'shoot' and 'dribble':

Q Why was the soccer player sent to jail?

A *For shooting.*

Q Why do babies make good soccer players?

A *They're great at dribbling.*

This flow chart also works for hobbies that use special
words; e.g. computers, music, cooking or animals.

CRAZY CACKLE-A-THON

Some of the best jokes are made from an unlikely and bizarre combination of things. Here are a couple of examples:

Q What has two horns and four wheels?

A *A cow on a skateboard.*

Q What is yellow and speeds?

A *A banana in a racing car.*

Why Do We Laugh?

So far, you've been learning how to write jokes using words that sound and look the same. But sometimes it's good to throw in a crazy joke every now and again – especially when your listeners aren't expecting it. Crazy jokes don't follow any of the rules we've been talking about. Crazy jokes put two different things together in a way that makes the punchline so bizarre that it's funny.

In the jokes we just read, the answers are both mad. You will never see a banana driving a racing car – or if you do, I suggest you keep well off the track. And if you see a cow in a skate park, steer clear of its back end!

With these jokes, you can let your imagination run wild. Why not try making some up yourself? They're easy and fun to write.

MAKE YOUR OWN
CRAZY JOKES

Make a list of animals and food – try two of each to start with. Call this 'List A'.

For example:

LIST A
Strawberry
Pig
Frog
Cake

Now write a list of four places you can go or things you can do. Call this 'List B'.

Here's an example:

LIST B
Drink a milkshake
Ride a bike
Have swimming lessons
Go parachuting

Think of a word or phrase to describe each word or phrase in Lists A and B. Call these new lists C and D.

For example:

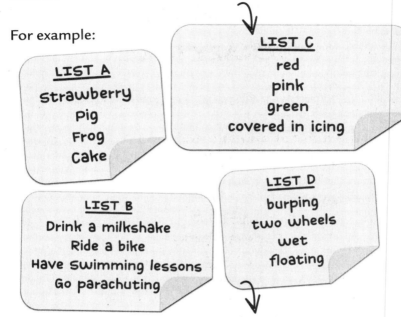

LIST C
red
pink
green
covered in icing

LIST A
Strawberry
Pig
Frog
Cake

LIST B
Drink a milkshake
Ride a bike
Have swimming lessons
Go parachuting

LIST D
burping
two wheels
wet
floating

The pattern for these jokes is: 'What is .... and ....?'

Use the describing words in your lists to fill in the gaps:

Q What is pink and burps?

A *A pig drinking a milkshake.*

Crazy Cackles

Q **What is yellow and wears a tie?**

A *A lemon in his best clothes.*

Q **What has 100 legs and pointy toes?**

A *A centipede doing ballet.*

Q **What has a long neck that goes up and down?**

A *A giraffe on a trampoline.*

Q **What is yellow and goes downhill fast?**

A *A banana on a water slide.*

Q **What is striped and lays eggs?**

A *A chicken in jail.*

more
chicken
jokes!!

CLOWNING AROUND

If you had a good sense of humour in the Middle Ages – and there probably wasn't much to laugh at in those days – your king might have given you the job of court jester.

A jester dressed in brightly coloured coats and leggings called 'motley', sometimes with a hood decorated to look like the head of a donkey or rooster. Bells were attached to his costume, his hood, and his long pointed shoes. He told jokes and played pranks to help the courtiers forget about their worries for a while.

I feel stupid!

Not So Foolish

Jesters were sometimes called 'fools', but most of the time they were clever and some even gave the king good advice.

One famous French jester named Jehan was called into court to sort out a problem between a baker and a porter. The baker was angry because the porter was sniffing his food. He thought the porter should have to pay for each sniff. Jehan the jester pretended to agree with the baker, then asked the porter to rattle the coins in his pocket. He told the baker that the sound of the coins paid for the smell of the food.

A Motley Crew

Chinese emperors first employed jesters 4000 years ago. In 300 BCE one jester managed to stop an emperor's plans to have the Great Wall of China painted with lacquer. The work was so dangerous that thousands of workers would have died. The jester joked about how long the project would take and the emperor gave up the idea.

Jesters were common in Europe, Great Britain, Japan, Russia, Africa, Persia and India until about 300 years ago.

Be Your Own Jester

Today, we could call a jester a stand-up comedian. Here are some ideas for building up your own comedy routine.

- Write a spoof of a nursery rhyme or a fairytale; perhaps you could swap bad characteristics for good ones, such as Little Red Riding Hood being a horrid girl who frightens the wolf.

- Write a Before or After version of a nursery rhyme or fairytale. For example, think of a funny reason why the Billy Goats Gruff needed to cross the bridge in the first place. Or choose a popular fairytale and think of a funny ending, instead of 'they lived happily ever after'.

- Do you play a musical instrument? Perhaps you could change the lyrics of popular songs to give your audience a surprise.

- Always carry a notebook to jot down funny ideas from daily life. Great ideas are all around – so keep your ears open on the bus, look at what people in the supermarket queue are buying, and use your imagination!

Send in the Clowns

Just as jesters joked with kings and courtiers, clowns cheered up crowds of ordinary people. And you still see clowns today. But unlike jesters, most clowns don't tell jokes. They make us laugh at their silly clothes and foolish behaviour.

In ancient Greece, clowns performed on stage after a serious drama, as an antidote to the tragedy of the play. They acted out a funny version and made all the heroes look like fools. Ancient Romans also used clowns in their plays. One character, known as Stupidus, always made mistakes. The other actors would pretend to get annoyed, knocking him around the stage to the delight of the audience.

Clowns travelled around from town to town to make their living, performing with acrobats, musicians and jugglers.

There were no stages, so clowns had to clear a space for the performance. Using a balloon on a stick, they hit people to keep them out of the performance area. Sometimes a clown would carry a broom and sweep people out of the way if they got too close to the actors.

Doctor Clown

Where is the most unlikely place you'd find a clown? A morgue? Or a hospital ward?

A movie starring Robin Williams tells the true story of how 'Patch' Adams was inspired to become a unique kind of clown-doctor through his own experiences in hospital. He used his clowning skills to help patients make a speedy recovery.

Clowning is now used in many hospitals around the world to help with the healing process. Professional clowns use juggling, mime, magic, jokes, funny hats and red noses, carrying rubber chickens instead of stethoscopes. Some doctors and nurses also dress up like clowns when they visit their patients.

Why Do We Laugh?

Researchers have come up with three different reasons why we laugh, and it's easy to see these at work when clowns perform.

The **Superiority Theory** suggests that we laugh at things that make us feel better than other people. Such as when a clown gets a pie in the face, falls off a chair or makes a silly mistake.

The **Incongruity Theory** says that when we see two things that don't normally go together, we laugh as a reaction to the shock or strangeness of the situation.

The **Relief Theory** says that people laugh as a way of coping with tension, and explains why comedians get lots of laughs from jokes about current world events such as political problems and food price rises.

You might feel inspired by the Superiority Theory to work out a routine based on slapstick, clumsy movements and other silliness that makes you look stupid. A lemon tart in the face or a collision with a door are always sure to get a laugh!

Or you could test the Incongruity Theory by putting weird things together – maybe a tutu with a chicken head!

INVENT-A-
WORD

Have you ever heard the word 'supercalifragilisticex-pialidocious'?

Some of the best words are the ones you make up yourself. Flummox your friends with wild and wondrous words – you might even start a trend at school. Or maybe some of your made-up words will become family favourites!

Q What ballet move do you perform in your sleep?

A *A pillowette.*

Q Where do bees go on Saturday nights?

A *A stingalong.*

Why Do We Laugh?

Invent-a-word jokes are funny because they change a familiar word into something new and odd. The real ballet move is called a 'pirouette'. By changing the sound slightly, you make a word that connects two seemingly unconnected things – ballet and sleep!

In the second joke, the term 'singalong' is altered slightly to give it an obvious connection with bees: 'stingalong'! Making up jokes like this can be easy.

Just change one part of a word and then come up with a question to fit the answer.

The key to a great invent-a-word joke is to make sure the sound of the made-up word is close enough to the sound of the real word for your listeners to make a connection straight away. The possibilities for made-up words are endless!

Say That Again?

Q What do mermaids have on toast?

A *Mermalade.*

Q What do you call a rude plane?

A *A swearaplane.*

Q What do you call a hippo with chicken pox?

A *A hippospotamus.*

Q How does a magician drink his tea?

A *From a cup and sorcerer.*

Q What kind of dog carries a disease?

A *Bacterrier.*

MAKE YOUR OWN
INVENT-A-WORD JOKES

Think of some interesting words with three or more syllables: food, musical instruments, animals, items of clothing, or anything else you like the sound of. If you're having trouble, use a dictionary.

Write down a few words. Call this 'List A'.

For example:

LIST A
Merry-go-round
saxophone
Alligator
Dictionary

Try to find a good rhyming word for the first one or two syllables of each word. Call this 'List B'.

35

For example:

> ## LIST B
>
> Merry rhymes with scary
> Sax rhymes with snacks
> Alli rhymes with smelly (almost!)
> Diction rhymes with fiction

Write a new list of made-up words using the rhyming words. Call this 'List C'.

For example:

> ## LIST C
>
> Scary-go-round
> Snaxophone
> Smellygator
> Fictionary

These new words are the punchlines for your jokes.

Link the real meaning of your original word with the meaning of the rhyming word to make a joke.

The jokes written from our list might look like this:

Q Which showground ride is more frightening than the Haunted House?

A *The scary-go-round.*

Q What musical instrument is the tastiest?

A *The snaxophone.*

Q What do you call an alligator with bad breath?

A *A smellygator.*

Q How do you find out the meanings of made-up words?

A *Look them up in a fictionary.*

Twisting Time

The jokes in the next workshop are similar to the ones on the previous pages. The only difference is that the punchlines in these jokes are real words with a new twist, instead of being made-up words.

Q What do you call a cow that is always sulking?

A *Moo-dy.*

Q What is the tastiest building in the world?

A *The Trifle Tower.*

Q What do you call the place where a UFO crashes?

A *Astroturf.*

Why Do We Laugh?

Remember the first rule of joke writing? Start at the end. The punchline in twister jokes is a word that has been given a new twist. All you need to do is find an interesting word and give it a new meaning.

In the first joke on the previous page, the word 'moody' starts with the sound made by a cow – MOO! In jokes like this, you need to make use of the true meaning of the whole word – moody – and the word contained within it – moo. So the joke had to be about a cow and it had to have something to do with a bad mood.

Tell her an udder joke

Compound words are also great for using in jokes because you can combine the two meanings.
A compound word is made up of two other words – like 'pitch/fork' or 'water/melon'

MAKE YOUR OWN
TWISTER JOKES

Write down a list of compound words (two words joined together), or other words that have more than one syllable. Call this 'List A'.

For example:

LIST A
Toadstool
Lollipop
Humble

These words are the punchlines for your jokes.

Now, separate the words or syllables within each of the entries on your list. Write the meaning, or meanings, of each word. Call this 'List B'.

For example:

LIST B

Toad   Frog
Stool Chair

Lolly Sweet for children
Pop   Modern music
       Soft drink
Hum   Not singing
ble   Bull

The pattern for these jokes is: 'What do you call ...?'

The words in List A form the punchline. Find a way to link the meanings of your List B words to form the joke.

Here are some examples:

   Q What do you call the place a frog sits to eat breakfast?

   A *A toadstool.*

Q What do you call sweet music?

A *Lollipop.*

Q What do you call a bull who won't sing?

A *Humble.*

Here are some examples:

Q What do you call a librarian who lives underground?

A *A bookworm.*

Q What do you call a pig with a skin problem?

A *Hogwarts.*

Q Where do you take sick horses?

A *Horse-pital.*

Q What do you call a baby chicken you buy at a garage sale?

A *Cheap.*

Q What do you call a group of people waiting to play pool?

A *A cue.*

Q What's the best place to store pork?

A *A piggy bank.*

PRANKS AND HOAXES

When you play a trick on someone, it's called a **practical joke**.

There's one day in the year when people expect to be tricked. The first day of April is known as April Fools' Day in many countries around the world.

Long ago, 1 April was the first day of the European year. In 1582 Pope Gregory XIII introduced a new calendar, called the Gregorian Calendar, which we still use today. The new calendar changed New Year's Day to 1 January, but news travelled slowly. People who didn't realise the calendar had been changed were called 'April fools' and other people played practical jokes on them. It wasn't long before 1 April was known throughout France, England and Scotland as a day for playing pranks such as sending people on fake errands, tying shoelaces together and giving silly gifts.

French victims of 1 April pranks are called *poisson d'avril*, which means 'April fish'. The name relates to how easy it is to catch newly hatched fish in April. French children take the joke further by taping pictures of fish to their friends' backs.

Scottish people prefer to attach 'kick me' signs to people's backs. They call 1 April 'Taily Day', when the jokes are all about backsides.

Sometimes television and radio stations play tricks on the public on April Fools' Day. One BBC television program convinced people that spaghetti grew on trees. Another tricked people into thinking that gravity would lessen on that day, meaning they could jump higher than usual – and even float around like astronauts!

Fool Your Friends

Here are some ideas for practical jokes you can play on your family and friends – but make sure everyone will end up laughing. Most practical jokes are harmless, but some can be dangerous. It's okay to put a whoopee cushion on someone's chair, but it's not safe to pull someone's chair out when they're about to sit down.

Practical jokes usually make the joker feel great, but the victim feels embarrassed at being fooled. If you're a practical joker, watch out! Some of your victims might want revenge!

Line a matchbox with cotton wool and puncture a hole in one end large enough to fit a thumb or finger through, concealing the hole with cotton. Stick your finger through the hole, adding some tomato sauce where your finger comes out of the cotton (don't overdo it!) to look like blood. Tell a friend you've found something gruesome and slide back the matchbox cover.

Put a spool of thread in your pocket that's the same colour as the garment, and leave the end of the thread hanging out. Then ask a friend or family member to help you break it off. When your friend tries to help by pulling it, it will go on and on and on and on!

Superglue some coins to the footpath, schoolground or any spot that has a lot of people walking about. Stand back and watch people break their fingernails trying to pick up the coins!

If the milk in your family's fridge comes in a carton that isn't see-through, add a few drops of food colouring.

Get up early to fetch the newspaper from the front doorstep. Replace the middle of today's paper with yesterday's paper. Your parent will become frustrated trying to find the rest of the cover story!

Put a whoopee cushion on your teacher's chair. Or hide it under a couch cushion to catch out members of your family.

An oldie but a goodie: open a door that you know someone will walk through and balance a pillow on top of it. When the person opens the door, the pillow will fall on their head.

Play an old Halloween game: prepare some bowls with boiled spaghetti (guts), chopped jelly (brains), blown-up rubber gloves (hands), peeled lychees or grapes (eyeballs) and so on. Blindfold a friend and ask them to guess which body parts they're feeling.

If the members of your family like to eat different types of cereal for breakfast, swap the bags inside with each other!

Hoaxes

Hoaxes are pranks that fool large numbers of people.
History records many famous hoaxes, some of which
have lasted for a long time. In the early 1900s, two
English girls aged ten and sixteen tricked the world
with photos of 'real' fairies. When they were old
women, they finally admitted the photos were of paper
cut-out fairies standing on hatpins!

Other famous hoaxes include the 1939 photo of
the Loch Ness Monster, which was revealed sixty years
later to have been a plastic head and neck mounted on
a toy submarine.

Orson Welles read out an extract from H.G. Wells's
book *The War of the Worlds* in a 1938 radio broadcast.
Many listeners panicked and fled from their homes,
believing they were being invaded by Martians.

Hugh's Hoaxes

Hugh Troy was an American university student in the
1920s who loved hoaxes. He found a rubbish bin made
out of a real rhinoceros foot. One snowy night he and
a friend filled the bin with weights and suspended it on
lines between them. They walked around the university
campus with the rhino foot, making prints in the snow.

Next morning, other students discovered the prints

leading to a hole in an ice-covered lake.

Because the lake was connected to the university's drinking supply, many people stopped drinking tap water. Others thought the water tasted of rhinoceros!

Troy would also visit New York's Central Park carrying a park bench he had bought. Police, suspecting he was stealing it, arrested him a number of times. He always presented the receipt and was released. Hugh took the prank further by organising a number of his friends to take park benches all at the same time. Because the police thought it was 'that guy with the bill of sale' again, none of the bench thieves were stopped as they walked out of the park.

Till's Trick

Till Eulenspiegel was a trickster who travelled throughout Germany during the 1300s. In one town he promised to paint a mural on a bare wall. The finished wall was still bare, but Till explained it had magical qualities. Only those with no secrets to hide could see the mural's beauty. Of course, no one wanted to admit they couldn't see anything, so everyone admired the wall. Till left town before people realised the truth.

ALL MIXED UP

Q What do you get when you cross a spider with an elephant?

A *Daddy-long-nose.*

Q What do you get when you cross a monkey with a flower?

A *A chimpansy.*

Why Do We Laugh?

These jokes mix things that don't usually go together: a spider and an elephant, or a monkey and a flower. The punchline in mixed-up jokes can be a made-up word or phrase – such as 'daddy-long-nose'. Or it can be a real word with a different spelling – like 'chimpansy'.

You can have a lot of fun with mixed-up jokes!

Mixed-up Madness

Q What do you get when you cross a large animal with perfume?

A *A smellyphant.*

Q What do you get when you cross a skeleton with a joke?

A *A funny bone.*

Q What do you get when you cross pasta with a question?

A *Spaguessi.*

Q What do you get when you cross a rabbit with a garden hose?

A *Hare spray.*

Q What do you get when you cross a giant gorilla with a skunk?

A *King pong.*

MAKE YOUR OWN
MIXED-UP JOKES

Make a list of animals, places, sayings, flowers and food. It's best to use compound words or longer phrases such as the ones below. Call this 'List A'.

For example:

LIST A
Baked Beans
Great Britain
Peanut Butter

Write a describing word for each word you have found. Call this 'List B'.

For example:

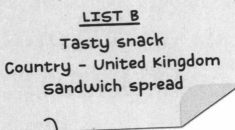

LIST B

Tasty snack
Country – United Kingdom
Sandwich spread

Choose one part of each word in List A and find a rhyme for it. Call this 'List C'.

For example:

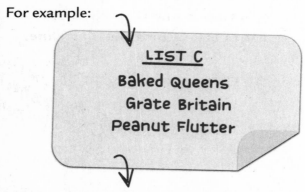

LIST C

Baked Queens
Grate Britain
Peanut Flutter

These words are the punchlines for your new jokes.

Look at your List C words. Think about how they have changed from your List A words. Write a describing phrase for that change. This is 'List D'.

For example:

> ### LIST D
> Queens — royalty
> Grate — cheese
> Flutter — butterfly

The pattern for these jokes is: 'What do you get when you cross a .... with a ....?'

Use the words in Lists B and D to fill in the gaps. The words in List C form the punchline.

Here are some examples:

Q What do you get when you cross a tasty snack with royalty?

A *Baked Queens.*

Q What do you get when you cross the United Kingdom with cheese?

A *Grate Britain.*

Q **What do you get when you cross a sandwich spread with a butterfly?**

A *Peanut Flutter.*

THE MISSING LINK

Q **Why is a magician like a cricket player?**

A *They both like doing hat tricks.*

Q **Why is a coat like a marathon runner?**

A *They both get worn out.*

Why Do We Laugh?

Missing-link jokes use double meanings to link two very different things and give them something in common. As usual, these jokes are written backwards and start with a good punchline.

A 'hat trick' is a cricketing term that means bowling three batsmen out in a row. But hat tricks for magicians are very different. And the phrase 'worn out' means one thing to a marathon runner and something else when used to describe a piece of clothing.

MAKE YOUR OWN
MISSING-LINK JOKES

Write a list of words or phrases that have more than one meaning. This is 'List A'.

For example:

LIST A
Trunk
Ring
Bee

These words are the punchlines for your new jokes.

Look at each of the words you have written in List A. For each word, write two things that are connected with that word. Call this 'List B'.

For example:

LIST B

Trunk   Elephant   Tree
Ring   Circus clown Finger
Bee   Flower   A, B, C

The pattern for these jokes is:
'Why is a .... like a ....?'

Use the List B words to fill the gaps in the question. The punchline starts with: 'They both ...'

Use the words in List A to complete the joke.

Here are some examples:

Q Why is an elephant like a tree?

A *They both have long trunks.*

Q **Why is a circus clown like a finger?**

A *They both look good in a ring.*

Q **Why is a flower like the letter A?**

A *A bee always comes after it.*

Still Missing

Q **Why is a manicurist like a secretary?**

A *They both do filing.*

Q **Why is a battery like a burglar?**

A *They both get charged.*

He.. He ..He..He...

Q **Why is a chicken like a broken toilet?**

A *They're both fowl.*

Q Why is a postcard like a rugby player who breaks the rules?

A *They both get sent off.*

Q Why is a newspaper like a tomato?

A *They're both red.*

Q Why is a pile of dirty dishes like a good basketball player?

A *No one likes to see them sitting on the bench.*

BRAIN TWISTERS

Have you ever found your tongue tangling over the words you want to say? Or had a completely different word pop out? Some people have actually become famous for it. It's even fun to do on purpose – the ancient art of wordplay, which includes riddles and tongue twisters, can really bend your brain!

I Hit My Bunny Phone

In the late 1800s and early 1900s a man named William Archibald Spooner taught at Oxford University in England. Spooner became famous for getting his words mixed up. Instead of saying 'lighting a fire', he would say 'fighting a liar'. And instead of telling a lazy student that he had 'wasted two terms', he said the young man had 'tasted two worms'. These mistakes soon became known as **spoonerisms**.

— What about forkerisms?

See if you can figure out what these spoonerisms really mean ...

- Go and shake a tower
- May I sew you to another sheet?
- A lack of pies
- You have mad banners
- Bred any good rooks lately?

... and make some more of your own!

A Pigment of Your Imagination

Richard Sheridan was a playwright in the 1700s. One of his plays, *The Rivals*, featured a character called Mrs Malaprop who used big words but often got them wrong. Instead of saying something was the 'pinnacle of politeness', she called it the 'pineapple of politeness'. Today, these slips of the tongue are called **malapropisms**.

Here are five malapropisms. See if you can work out what the speaker really meant to say:

- I got stuck in the revolting doors.
- Flying saucers are an optical conclusion.
- The flood damage was so bad they had to evaporate the city.
- He used a fire distinguisher to put out the flames.
- She starts on one subject, then goes off on a tandem.

What malapropisms can you come up with?

Oxymoronic

If you listen closely when people speak, you'll notice some strange word combinations. Ever described someone as 'pretty ugly'? 'Pretty' and 'ugly' are opposites – yet we use phrases like that all the time. Another example is 'seriously funny'. They're called **oxymorons** – which is a seriously funny word in itself! Here are some more:

- Simply impossible
- Original copy
- Almost exactly
- Same difference

Playing with Words

Mixing up words and letters accidentally is one thing. It's quite another thing to do it deliberately, such as when you get tangled up in a **tongue twister**. When we do that, it's called **wordplay** – and all you need for wordplay is a piece of paper and a pencil!

People have been playing with their words for thousands of years. Three other forms of wordplay that are fun to play with are **anagrams**, **palindromes** and **riddles**.

Do you sometimes have trouble finding exactly the right word? That's because there are so many to choose from. There are more than 600 000 words in the English language and hundreds more are added each year. Perhaps that's why it's so easy to make a slip of the tongue. It's hard for our brains to keep up with it all!

Pickled Peppers

Ever been tongue-tied? Maybe someone asked you to repeat a tongue twister.

Most people have heard of Peter Piper. He's the guy who picked a peck of pickled peppers. (Say it really fast: *Peter Piper picked a peck of pickled peppers.*)

Tongue twisters are sentences that repeat the same starting sound and are tricky to get your tongue around. It's easy to say a tongue twister slowly. But the faster you get and the more often you say it, the more likely you are to get mixed up – sometimes with hilarious results! The more you practise, the better you'll be at tongue twisters. In fact, 'practice makes perfect' works as its own tongue twister: try it and see!

Here's another funny tongue twister:

A skunk sat on a stump
And thunk the stump stunk
But the stump thought the skunk stunk.

Anagram Antics

Anagrams are made by mixing up the letters of words or phrases to make new words or phrases. A simple example is changing 'spare' to 'pears'. All the letters are still there in the second word; they're just in a different order.

Some very clever people even manage to make up anagrams that seem to relate to the original word. Two clever anagrams are 'moon starer', which is an anagram of 'astronomer', and 'nine thumps', which is an anagram of 'punishment'. You need plenty of time and patience to create anagrams like that, but it's still lots of fun to mix up letters in words and phrases and see what happens.

Try making new phrases using your own name as well as the names of your friends and family. I played around with the letters in my name and came up with 'thrash loon'. I hope you have better luck with the letters in your name!

Pop a Palindrome

Think about the words 'mum' and 'dad'. If you look closely, you'll see that both words read the same backwards and forwards. Words like these are called palindromes. Other everyday examples of palindromes are 'eye', 'pop', 'level' and 'madam'.

Palindromes become really interesting when more than one word is used. The most well-known example of a palindrome phrase is probably 'Madam, I'm Adam'. As long as you don't worry too much about the punctuation, that phrase reads exactly the same whether you start at the beginning or the end. Another well-known palindrome is 'Do geese see God?'

Riddle Me This

There was once a green house. Inside the green house was a white house. Inside the white house was a red house. Inside the red house were lots of babies. What was it?

This is an ancient wordplay called a riddle. Did you work it out? The answer is *a watermelon*.

Riddles have been around for thousands of years. One of the oldest and most famous riddles is the riddle of the Sphinx, a legendary winged monster that tormented the Theban people of ancient Greece. The Sphinx killed everyone who couldn't answer its riddle. Finally, a hero called Oedipus solved the riddle and the Sphinx killed itself.

Let's see how well you would have done if you were a Theban living in ancient Greece:

What goes on four legs in the morning, two legs in the daytime and three legs in the evening?

The answer to the riddle of the Sphinx is man. He crawls on four legs as an infant, walks on two legs as an adult and uses a walking stick (a third leg) in his old age.

Here are some riddles for you to try out on your friends.

Q I give away my first letter. I give away my second letter. I give away all my letters. Who am I?

A *A postman.*

Q What is as light as air but can't be held for long?

A *Your breath.*

Q What gets lost every time you stand up?

A *Your lap.*

Q Is it more correct to say 'the yolk of the egg is white' or 'the yolk of an egg are white'?

A *Neither. The yolk of an egg is yellow.*

LAUGHERS
LAST LONGER

Have you heard that 'laughter is the best medicine'?
No one's quite sure who said it first, but it probably
comes from an old Bible verse that reads: 'A merry
heart does good like a medicine, but a broken spirit
dries the bones'.

And it's true! As well as giving your muscles a workout,
laughter helps you fight disease. It triggers chemicals
that make you feel good, stay alert, remember more
and feel creative. What's more, your brain can't tell
the difference between real and fake laughter – so your
body can benefit even if you have nothing to smile
about. Try chuckling anyway!

A Chuckle a Day Can ...

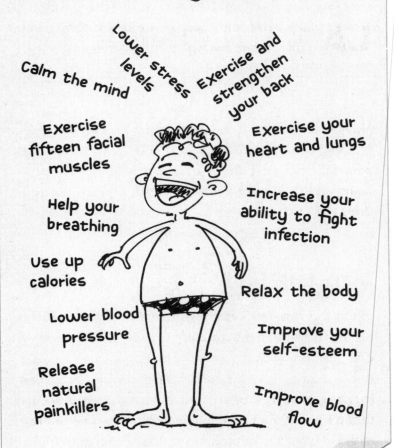

Lower stress levels

Calm the mind

Exercise and strengthen your back

Exercise fifteen facial muscles

Exercise your heart and lungs

Help your breathing

Increase your ability to fight infection

Use up calories

Relax the body

Lower blood pressure

Improve your self-esteem

Release natural painkillers

Improve blood flow

Many ancient cultures knew that laughter could help sick people. One South American rainforest tribe held laughter festivals to help sick people recover more quickly. And centuries ago in Asia, doctors were known to encourage their patients to laugh when things weren't going well.

Join the Club

In 1995, Dr Madan Kataria was researching an article on the health benefits of laughter when he woke up one morning with the idea of starting a laughter club. If it is so good for you, he thought, why not get more people chuckling? He started a small club in India and told jokes for the first few meetings. When he ran out of good gags, Dr Kataria taught yoga and breathing techniques to get people laughing. The idea proved so popular that it has spread to more than 2500 laughter clubs throughout the world.

In 1998, the first World Laughter Day was held. This day is now celebrated each year on the first Sunday in May. In 2000, on World Laughter Day in Denmark, 8200 people laughed their way into the Danish pages of the Guinness World Records for the most people laughing together without reason.

Getting the Giggles

Like yawning, laughter can be catching. Researchers have discovered that the brain has a special detector that reacts to laughter. When we hear someone else giggling, the detector triggers other parts of our brain so that we giggle too. That's why laugh tracks or 'canned' laughter are used on TV comedy shows.

Witty Words of Wisdom

I am thankful for laughter, except when milk comes out of my nose. Woody Allen

Laughter is the shortest distance between two people. Victor Borge

Seven days without laughter make one weak. Joel Goodman

Laughter is an instant vacation.
Milton Berle

A good time for laughing is when you can. Jessamyn West

Laughter is the sun that drives winter from the human face.
Victor Hugo

A clown is like aspirin, only he works twice as fast. Groucho Marx

At the height of laughter, the universe is flung into a kaleidoscope of new possibilities.
Jean Houston

Funny is an attitude.
Flip Wilson

He who laughs, lasts.
Mary Pettibone Poole

Laughter is a tranquilliser with no side effects. Arnold Glasgow

Laughter is part of the human survival kit. David Nathan

THE LAST LAUGH

I hope you've enjoyed reading jokes, writing jokes and learning about how to make your family and friends laugh. Remember to keep smiling, laugh a lot and see the funny side of life as often as possible. It really helps! And, to send you on your way, here are some of my favourite jokes to share with your friends.

Q How do you make up a joke?

A *A good foundation and a lot of lippy.*

Q Why did the man sleep under the car?

A *He wanted to wake up oily in the morning.*

Q Why couldn't the egg finish telling jokes?

A *He kept cracking up.*

Knock knock
Who's there?
Mr Bean.
Mr Bean who?
**Mr Bean standing here
for ten minutes already.**

— Just wait there for the time bean.

Q **What did the auctioneer say
when he sold the pair of cymbals?**

A *Going, going, gong.*

Q **What did the mother say when her
son got pins and needles in his hands?**

A *Good. You can sew the buttons on this shirt.*

Q **Why was the alien looking
for a gardening job?**

A *He had green fingers.*

Q **What is put on a table, cut,
but never eaten?**

A *A deck of cards.*

Knock knock
Who's there?
Ya.
Ya who?
Keep the noise down, will you?

**Q What did the astrologer say
to the vampire?**

A *Let me write your horrorscope.*

**Q What do dogs do
when they agree on something?**

A *Shake on it.*

Knock knock
Who's there?
Otter.
Otter who?
**Otter brush your hair
before you open the
door next time.**

Q What do you call a girl
with a sweet tooth?

A *Candy.*

Knock knock
Who's there?
Royal.
Royal who?
Royal be round later. I'm Tim.

Q What can you break just by speaking?

A *Silence.*

Knock knock
Who's there?
Chicken.
Chicken who?
**Chicken side and see if
I left my keys on the table,
will you?**

Q Why didn't the oyster have any friends?

A *He was too shellfish.*

Q Why did the truck driver stop for a meal?

A *Because he came to a fork in the road.*

Q What card game do crocodiles play?

A *Snap.*

Get the cards and make it snappy!

Q I run, yet have no legs. What am I?

A *A nose.*

Q Why was the dog's surprise party ruined?

A *Because someone let the cat out of the bag.*

Q What did the coach say to the player who kept complaining that his boots were too big?

A *Put a sock in it.*

Q **Why did the worm lose the court case?**

A *He didn't have a leg to stand on.*

Q **What did the number three say to the number four?**

A *I'll get even with you if it's the last thing I do.*

Q **Tear off my skin, and I won't cry, but you will. What am I?**

A *An onion.*

Q **Where do umpires hold their meetings?**

A *The Umpire State Building.*

Q **Where is the deepest point of the ocean?**

A *On the bottom.*

Q Why did the chicken lay an egg?

A *So the pig didn't have to.*

Q Brothers and sisters have I none, but that man's father is my father's son. Who is he?

A *My son.*

Q Why did the boy smash all the clocks in the morning?

A *His mother told him to kill some time before school.*

Q A bucket of water weighs ten kilograms. What should you add to it to make it weigh five kilograms?

A *Holes.*

Q The more you take, the more you leave behind. What are they?

A *Footsteps.*

Q **Why did the barber leave his job?**

A *He'd had too many close shaves.*

Q **What lives all alone in a dwelling with no doors or windows, and can only leave by breaking through the wall?**

A *A chicken in an egg.*

SHARON HOLT laughs a lot, but she can't remember the punchlines of any jokes. She doesn't like pranks and hoaxes, thinks clowns are overrated and is hopeless at tongue twisters. Despite all this, she figured out how jokes work, wrote a book about it and found a publisher – which gave her a lot to smile about.

Now she has great fun writing books from her home in Kihikihi, which she shares with her husband Alan, two children named Gregory and Sophie, a cat named Moose and a goldfish named Killa.

ROSS KINNAIRD loves jokes. This got him into trouble at school. Now his ability at maths is truly funny. He is emperor, president and sole member of the International League of Chicken Jokers. (Please note that all hate mail from chickens will be passed on to the proper authorities … he does not find this amusing.)

Ross lives in Auckland and when he is not busy drawing funny pictures, he is usually found crossing the road to get to the other side.

LIKE ALL BOOKS, this book is the collaborative effort of many people.

Firstly, thanks to my children Gregory and Sophie, whose attempts at humour inspired me to figure out how jokes work.

My husband Alan was very supportive over the time it took to get this book finished – and even helped write some of the jokes.

Other jokes were written by children and teachers from Puahue School and Korakonui School. They graciously allowed me to come into their classrooms and use them as guinea pigs in the joke writing process.

The research needed to write this book was made much easier thanks to my local Te Awamutu librarians, headed by the tireless Sheree. Thanks again, ladies.

My agents at Richards Literary Agency made this book possible by finding a publisher who loved the idea as much as I did.

The contributions of Hilary Reynolds, Eva Mills and Sarah Brenan at Allen & Unwin have been outstanding. I have appreciated your encouragement, support and magical ability to turn too many words into just the right amount.

And, last but not least, a big thank you must go to Ross Kinnaird for bringing my jokes to life with his hilarious cartoons.

Sharon Holt